THE INNKEEPER'S JOURNAL

A Christmas Classic

Raymond McHenry

Illustrated by
Matthew Chandler

INTERNATIONAL

Cover Illustration by Loyd Fannin

Hardcover 978-1-7327180-0-5

Also available in Spanish

Printed in the USA

To Jesus Christ,

who came to give us life as God intended

From the Author

The *Innkeeper's Journal* is an imaginative story that provides a fresh perspective on Christmas for people of all ages. It's designed to be read at family gatherings, so the pages are filled with colorful pictures to keep children engaged while teenagers and adults listen to a parable-like story filled with opportunities for spiritual growth and maturity.

In Luke 2:7, the Bible tells us that when Mary and Joseph arrived in Bethlehem "there was no room for them in the inn." From that scant piece of information, countless Christmas pageants have included a nameless innkeeper repeating those memorable words, "No room!"

This fictional story builds on Luke's historical footnote and envisions what might have happened if the innkeeper's storyline continued long after that unforgettable night in Bethlehem. What if his entire life was affected more than we've ever imagined?

We generally remember the basic details surrounding Jesus' birth, but that common familiarity can hinder our understanding of what Christmas is all about. The innkeeper's character, "Jedidiah," reminds us why Jesus came to Earth.

Because this story merges facts with fiction, I included my personal notes at the back of this book to help guide the reader. This section offers more insights regarding the biblical references scattered throughout the story and should facilitate further reading and study. It also contains discussion questions to use with your family and/or a small group.

The full account of what happened when Jesus was born can be found in the New Testament books of Matthew and Luke. I suggest reading the first two chapters in both of these books as part of your Christmas tradition.

This story really inspired me as I wrote it. I hope it inspires you as you read it.

With Gratitude,
Raymond

Introduction

W hat if the innkeeper's storyline continued long after that unforgettable night in Bethlehem when he turned away Joseph and Mary? What if his experience with Jesus helps us better understand the real meaning of Christmas?

The Innkeeper's Journal takes you on a riveting and surprising ride through the life of a man who has much more to tell us than, "No room in the inn."

It only takes ten minutes to read, but this short story may permanently change the way you look at Christmas.

THE INNKEEPER'S JOURNAL

My name is Jedidiah, which means *loved by the Lord*, and that's an important part of this story. I was named after King David's favored son because our family has lived in Bethlehem for generations, and this city has a strong connection with Israel's mighty leader.

I'm not actually mentioned in the Bible. Dr. Luke just stated that we didn't have room in the inn for Mary and Joseph. Most people think I'm a heartless footnote in history, but that's not entirely true, so thank you for taking another look at my story.

About forty years ago I took over the inn for my father. Neither of my older brothers wanted to be a village innkeeper, so they moved a few miles north to the big city of Jerusalem and left me with the family business.

When you live in a small town like ours, taking care of an inn doesn't produce much money. Most people stay with relatives when they visit, so it's a tough way to make a living.

When Caesar Augustus issued his decree for a worldwide census, I started seeing real financial possibilities. Bethlehem had been around for 1,300 years so plenty of people have deep family roots here. And sure enough, the town filled up fast. In fact, it was the first time our inn had ever been full.

As you might expect, I was very busy and preoccupied. I had to make sure everyone had a place to stay, collect all of the lodging fees, and then guard the purse because it was more money than I'd ever seen.

Everything was going just fine until that couple from Nazareth showed up. I was uncomfortable that we didn't have a decent place left for a pregnant woman, but we were completely full and I was worn out. Innkeepers are typically quite hospitable, but that night, all I wanted to do was crawl in bed and go to sleep.

Now I know what you're thinking, "Why didn't you let her stay in your house?" Well, my home was already filled with extended family and to top it off, my wife, Ruth, was pregnant. It was early in the process so she was sick much of the time. I couldn't handle any more guests in our little cottage so I gave them the only spot available, the stable. I made sure they had everything they needed and then called it a night.

You obviously know how it all played out. Sure enough, she had her baby right there in the barn. But she never complained. Her husband, Joseph, was a very creative guy. He didn't have anything like a crib so he cleaned out the feed trough, put in some fresh hay, and laid his son in that manger. I was quite impressed with his ingenuity.

*L*ater that night, strange things started taking place. The sky became incredibly bright with this amazing star, and you could hear singing that was absolutely heavenly. Around midnight some shepherds came running in claiming that an angel told them this baby was the Son of God. Normally you can't trust shepherds, but what they had to say was very convincing. We even heard that wise men from the east were on their way to worship this child who was out in my barn.

It was all so surreal. I wondered if this was really happening. Could it be that the prophecy of Micah was actually being fulfilled? Was this truly the Messiah? And was he literally born behind my house? It's what I hoped and believed for the next two years, until everything changed.

There are certain days you never forget and this was that day. You could see dust on the horizon as a centurion led his troops toward our city. That wasn't terribly uncommon, but it did seem like a lot of soldiers for our small community.

When the Romans arrived, they ordered everyone to the town square. Again, that wasn't unusual so we gathered up our families and came together. We figured it must be another part of the census or some new demand Rome was always making.

But this time they ordered us to bring out all of the boys who were two years of age or younger. That seemed odd, but we did what they commanded.

Then, in a moment, it happened. My Micaiah and two-dozen other little boys were gone. Those despised Romans ruthlessly ended their lives and then just marched out of town.

In fewer than twenty minutes my whole life changed. We had read those prophetic words of Jeremiah many times concerning great sorrow in the City of David, but none of us ever dreamed we would be the ones in Bethlehem weeping for our children and refusing to be comforted.

I had named Micaiah after that fearless prophet in the Old Testament who never cowered from speaking the truth. Everyone knew a great ruler would again come from Bethlehem, so I prayed for God to make Micaiah a mighty leader. But now…I was holding the lifeless form of my little son…wrapped in swaddling clothes…and laying him in a grave next to our stable.

We later discovered this all happened because Herod was afraid of that child who was born at our inn. But the baby boy that was wrapped in swaddling clothes and laid in a manger in my barn wasn't here. He had long since left Bethlehem. He didn't die! But my Micaiah did!

Today I curse God

and hope to die

I knew then and there that he wasn't the Messiah. If he were, this wouldn't have happened. I had always been a God-fearing man, but no more. That day I wrote in my journal, *"Today I curse God and hope to die!"*

After seeing what happened to my only child, I understood exactly what Job's wife meant when she saw her husband's great suffering and yelled, "Curse God and die!" I felt the same as Naomi when she returned to Bethlehem from Moab after losing her husband and two sons. She told her friends to quit calling her Naomi and start calling her Mara because she was bitter.

That was me. I was a bitter man and stayed that way for thirty years. Ruth and I never had another child so I guess it's pretty remarkable we stayed married. We were just two hollow people that made more sense together than apart.

After three decades of miserable existence, a tiny spark flickered in my soul. This well-known rabbi stopped by the inn and asked if we could talk. His name was Jesus and everybody knew about him. He performed miracles and taught like nobody we'd ever heard. I was honored that he came to my house, but I honestly wasn't interested in hearing about God.

Then he asked me an unusual question. He wanted to know if he could look at my stable. It seemed odd to me, but who was I to tell this great teacher he couldn't see my barn?

When we got back there, he told me a strange but familiar story. He explained how he was the baby born there thirty-three years ago. When I heard this, I sensed a change within me. It was like my heart softened for the first time in decades.

He left and headed toward Jerusalem with this fire in his eyes and a deep sense of peace.

Not long afterwards, I was in Jerusalem and saw something that brought me back to that horrible day in Bethlehem. The Romans killed him too! That glimmer of hope, that he might be the One, was dashed. It was as devastating as the day my little Micaiah died. The darkness of my soul seemed overwhelming, until I heard something that was as wild as the night he was born.

People were claiming an angel said that Jesus was alive. I couldn't imagine it being true because I saw him die, but something inside of me wanted to believe it. So I went and found his disciples. They were ecstatic! All of them kept talking at the same time, and they couldn't stop laughing. Finally, Peter said, "Thomas, you tell him." Thomas explained how he didn't believe it either, but then he saw Jesus and touched his wounds. He shouted, "HE'S ALIVE!"

A few weeks later I was with a crowd of about 500 people, which is more people than live in my village, and Jesus was there. He really was alive...and still is!

I knelt before Jesus and received him as my Lord and Savior. His disciples baptized me, and then I went back home and told Ruth. For the first time since that day we lost Micaiah, I saw her come back to life. She claimed Christ as her Lord too, and because we were the first believers in Bethlehem, we started a church. It wasn't in our house like most churches. It was in our stable. Yep, we went back to that old barn and worshiped the One who was born there—the One Isaiah described as Wonderful, Counselor, Mighty God, Everlasting Father, Prince of Peace.

Each time we go back there to worship God, we pass by our little Micaiah's grave. Rather than being filled with bitterness and grief like we were before, we now say in the City of David what the great king said after his son died, "I will go to him one day."

Right after David said those words, the Bible explains that he soon had another son. The prophet Nathan declared his name would be Jedidiah because it would remind David and Bathsheba that even though they had sinned, they were still loved by God. That's why Jesus came, to demonstrate this truth to us all.

You probably remember Jedidiah as Solomon, and that's a good thing. The name Solomon comes from Shalom, which means *peace*. But it means much more than we often think. Shalom is the peace of God and it means *life as God intended*. Jesus was born in my barn so you and I could experience life as He intended.

Tragedy, disappointment, disbelief and disillusionment are NEVER evidence against God. Therefore ALWAYS pray, trust, and hope in Him.

Jedidiah

S o take it from my journal and me. Here's what I wrote after I met the risen Lord:

"Tragedy, disappointment, disbelief, and disillusionment are NEVER evidence against God. Therefore, ALWAYS pray, trust, and hope in Him."

Because of Jesus, I'm living life as God intended...and so can you!

How to Experience Life as God Intended

Jedidiah is a fictional character in this story, but he represents what all of us can truly experience with God. If you would like to have your life changed like his, act upon these truths from the Bible.

★ **God loves you more than you can imagine, and He created you to have an eternal and abundant relationship with Him.** The best-known verse in the Bible is John 3:16, and it tells of God's great love for you. Jesus said, "My purpose is to give life in all its fullness" (John 10:10). Second Corinthians 9:15 talks about God's desire for us to have His "indescribable gift" of love and forgiveness through Jesus Christ. And John 17:3 defines eternal life as the privilege of knowing God—having an eternal and abundant relationship with Him.

★ **But there's a horrible problem...Our sin prevents us from having any relationship with God.** The Old and New Testaments of the Bible tell us the same thing...our sin separates us from God (Isaiah 59:2 and Romans 3:23) and makes us enemies of God (Romans 5:10 and Colossians 1:21).

★ **Thankfully, Jesus can make us right with God.** In John 14:6 Jesus declared His exclusive and victorious role as humanity's Savior: "I am the way, the truth, and the life. No one comes to the Father except through me."

★ **We can be changed for eternity by crying out to God in prayer and humbly repenting of our sins.** In the New Testament book of Luke, Jesus describes what it takes to be saved from our sins: "God, have mercy on me, a sinner" (Luke 18:13). Repenting of our sins involves the complete surrender of our life to Christ. Jesus said, "If any of you wants to be my follower, you must turn from your selfish ways, take up your cross daily, and follow me" (Luke 9:23).

★ **You can begin an eternal and abundant relationship with God and start experiencing life as God intended with an initial prayer like this:** Lord Jesus, I recognize I am a sinner in desperate need of your forgiveness. Please forgive me of all my sins and become the Lord and Savior of my life. I surrender to you all that I am and all that I have, and I will follow hard after you the remaining days of my one and only life. Amen!

The Bible tells us, "Those who become a Christian become a new person" (2 Corinthians 5:17). If you just asked Jesus to forgive you of your sins and be the Lord of your life, you are now 1) a brand-new person in Christ, and 2) a member of God's eternal family (John 1:12).

To grow and mature as a Christian: a) read the Bible daily—the Gospel of Luke is a great place to begin; b) speak to God regularly in prayer—it's a conversation where you both talk and listen; c) get baptized and become a fully engaged member in a church that affirms the Lordship of Jesus Christ and the authority of the Bible; d) tell everyone about God's great love and forgiveness that's been demonstrated through Jesus Christ (Romans 5:8).

Discussion Questions

1) Which parts of Jedidiah's story do you like best and why?

2) What parts of Jedidiah's life do you relate to the most? Explain.

3) How has this short story changed your thoughts about Christmas?

4) Are you more like Jedidiah before or after he was changed by Jesus? Explain.

5) When was a time you allowed disappointment, disbelief, disillusionment, or tragedy to make you bitter towards God? How did you overcome that?

6) Jedidiah wrote in his journal, "ALWAYS pray, trust, and hope in Him." How is that similar or different from your perspective on life?

7) Jedidiah means *loved by the Lord*. Do you feel that's true in your life? Why or why not?

8) Solomon's name reminds us that true peace is living life as God intended. How often do you currently experience that kind of peace? Explain.

9) Think about the titles and roles describing Jesus in Isaiah 9:6—*Wonderful, Counselor, Mighty God, Everlasting Father, Prince of Peace*. Which ones do you like best or need most right now?

10) Have you committed your life to Jesus Christ like Jedidiah did (page 49), or are you still in the process of making that commitment?

Notes on the Story

Because this story merges facts with fiction, these notes are provided to help guide the reader. This section offers clarity and insights regarding the biblical references made throughout the story and can be used for further reading and study.

The full account of what happened when Jesus was born can be found in the New Testament books of Matthew and Luke. I recommend reading the first two chapters in both of these books as part of your Christmas tradition.

King David had numerous sons, but Solomon was the one chosen to be his successor. The prophet Nathan named him Jedidiah in 2 Samuel 12:24-25 because God wanted to send a clear message that he and his parents were *loved by the Lord.*

In Jesus' time most trades and livelihoods were passed down from generation to generation so it would be quite natural for the innkeeper's son to take over the family business. Since most travelers stayed in homes, running an inn was seldom a lucrative vocation because it typically meant providing lodging just for visitors who had no relatives in town.

The Roman Empire took a census about every fourteen years, and all men were required to return to the city of their birth. The objective was to assess taxes and locate males who could be forced into military service. Since the Jews were exempt from the military, Rome's focus in Israel was strictly monetary. This mandated census meant the city would be filled to capacity and the inn would run out of room, just like the Gospel of Luke records.

★

It's quite likely the innkeeper was stretched to the point of exhaustion, yet his propensity for hospitality could have very well led him to open the stable as a preferred option over staying in his courtyard or the town square.

The details of that night are significant. We typically think of a manger as a stable, but mangers were actually the feed troughs from which animals ate. Shepherds weren't respected or considered trustworthy. Courts wouldn't even accept a shepherd's testimony because people deemed them dishonest. God chose a group of so-called liars to herald the truth of Christ's birth, which says a lot about the love and grace of God. And it reminds us that God doesn't require perfect conditions to accomplish his plans. It's quite an irony that the Creator would come to his Creation under these conditions.

Information about the wise men can be found in Matthew 2:1-15. Their arrival probably didn't occur until sometime later after Jesus' birth. This explains why Herod ordered the execution of all the boys two years of age and younger.

The Old Testament book of Micah refers to the Messiah being born in Bethlehem. Micah 5:2 states, "But you, Bethlehem Ephrathah, though you are small among the clans of Judah, out of you will come for me one who will be ruler over Israel, whose origins are from old, from ancient times."

★

Herod's order to execute the boys two years of age and younger in Bethlehem and its vicinity is recorded in the New Testament book of Matthew (2:13-18). The estimation of two dozen boys was based on the town's actual population of around 300 people. The details of how this great tragedy took place are not certain, but it could have easily occurred the way it's described.

The Old Testament book of Jeremiah predicted Herod's murderous rampage. Jeremiah 31:15 states, "A voice is heard in Ramah, mourning and great weeping, Rachel weeping for her children and refusing to be comforted, because her children are no more."

King Herod was a paranoid leader who regularly murdered any perceived threat to his throne, so his order to exterminate the baby boys in Bethlehem was in keeping with his ruthless character. Through a dream, an angel warned Joseph of Herod's intent so he took Jesus and Mary to Egypt for protection (Matthew 2:13-15).

The meaning behind the name of Jedidiah's son, Micaiah, is as described. He was truly a fearless prophet who never cowered from speaking the truth. His story of courage can be read in the following two Old Testament books: 1 Kings 22 and 2 Chronicles 18.

The burial process in ancient times was similar to what is written. Jedidiah would have wrapped his son in cloth much like baby Jesus was wrapped in swaddling clothes. An example of this process can be seen in the New Testament book of John (19:38-42) where Jesus' burial is described. The correlation is significant. Jesus and the fictional character of Jedidiah's son, Micaiah, were both wrapped in swaddling clothes when they were born, and both were buried in much the same way.

The heartbreaking sorrow of Jedidiah led to his disillusionment with God. He felt an immediate bond with Job's wife who angrily lashed out at her husband in their great loss and demanded that he "Curse God and die!" (Job 2:9). The Old Testament book of Job describes the horrors this couple faced in the first two chapters (Job 1-2).

Since the story of Jedidiah takes place in Bethlehem, all those who lived there would readily recall the history of Naomi. She was a well-known resident from their ancient past because she was the mother-in-law of King David's great-grandmother Ruth. Naomi experienced the loss of her husband and two sons while living in the land of Moab. When she returned to Bethlehem as a widow and brokenhearted mother, she told her friends and relatives to call her Mara, which means bitter. Naomi's words of grief can be read in the Old Testament book of Ruth: "Call me Mara (which means bitter), because the Almighty has made my life very bitter" (Ruth 1:20). Jedidiah and his wife, Ruth, had that same sense of bitterness after losing their only child.

The meeting of Jedidiah and Jesus at the inn before Jesus was crucified in Jerusalem is not in the Bible. It was written to communicate how the power of Christ can change anyone's life.

The crucifixion and resurrection of Jesus are both historical facts. The first four books of the New Testament are called Gospels, which means "good news." Jesus' crucifixion and resurrection are definitely good news for us, and the four Gospels all contain detailed accounts of these two eternally significant events.

The Bible repeatedly addresses Jesus' crucifixion and resurrection because they are the central message of Scripture. You can read the full account in the final chapters of each Gospel: Matthew 26-28; Mark 14-16; Luke 22-24 and John 18-21. More details can be found in these New Testament books: Acts 1:1-3; Romans 1:4; 1 Corinthians 15:1-58; Philippians 2:5-11; 1 Peter 2:24; Revelation 1:5 & 18.

The scene where Jedidiah meets the disciples after Jesus' resurrection merges truth and imagination. Jedidiah is a fictional character, but the disciples were truly changed men after Jesus came back to life. Then they literally changed the world.

The New Testament book of John details how Jesus met with his disciples and invited Thomas, who had doubts, to examine the wounds in his hands, feet, and side. That encounter permanently changed Thomas and eradicated his doubts. Read about it in John 20:24-31. It's easy to believe the disciples were filled with laughter, and that's suggested in Luke 24:41 where it speaks of their "joy and amazement."

The New Testament book of 1 Corinthians devotes an entire chapter to the historical resurrection of Jesus Christ (Chapter 15). In 1 Corinthians 15:6, the Apostle Paul writes that Jesus was seen by more than 500 of his followers at one time. Although Jedidiah is a fictional character, that large gathering 2,000 years ago with the resurrected Lord actually happened.

Through the centuries, billions of people have experienced the kind of change described in Jedidiah. Each transformed person has done what the story says of Jedidiah: they humbled themselves before Christ and acknowledged Him as Lord and Savior. They were then baptized and became active members of a local church that perpetually worships Christ as the only One who can save us from our sin.

It was several centuries after Christ that Christians started constructing church buildings. Prior to that, followers of Jesus worshiped in homes. It would not be unusual for a character like Jedidiah to use his stable as a place for Christians to come together and worship Jesus. A church was constructed in the 4th century A.D. to mark the traditional site of Jesus' birth, and the Church of the Nativity is at that location today.

Jedidiah's reference to Christ as, "Wonderful, Counselor, Mighty God, Everlasting Father,

Prince of Peace" comes from the Old Testament book of Isaiah (9:6). These five titles are beautiful descriptions of Jesus and his work. Some Bible translations do not include a comma between Wonderful and Counselor, but it can be translated either way. The comma is included here to reveal that Jesus is Wonderful, and he's a wonderful Counselor.

The transformative change you see in Jedidiah and his wife is common among Christians who truly seek God with all of their heart, soul, and mind (Matthew 22:37-40). Few things in life hurt more than the loss of a child, yet countless heartbroken parents have put their trust in Christ and discovered that the only cure for bitterness and grief is found in God (2 Corinthians 1:3-4).

Jedidiah's reference to King David losing an infant son can be found in the Old Testament book of 2 Samuel. That baby boy, who was born to Bathsheba as a result of their adulterous relationship, lived just one week. After he died, David declared, "I will go to him, but he will not return to me" (2 Samuel 12:23). David understood that there is life beyond the grave. Everyone who embraces Christ has the opportunity to be reunited in Heaven.

The crushing blow of David and Bathsheba burying their first child together was followed by the birth of Solomon. The prophet Nathan called him Jedidiah, and even though that wasn't the name his parents used, it served as a powerful reminder of God's love. In the Old Testament book of 2 Samuel we see that Jedidiah means *loved by God* (2 Samuel 12:24-25).

The other name given to David and Bathsheba's son carries equally significant meaning. The name Solomon comes from Shalom, which translates as *peace*. This kind of peace means much more than the absence of conflict. Shalom means *life as God intended*. Jesus came to live, die, and be resurrected so that we can have a relationship with him and experience life as he intended—"life in all its fullness" (John 10:10 NLT).

The fictional character of Jedidiah spent much of his life hollowed out with bitterness toward God. Once he understood who Jesus really was, the Son of God, this bitter innkeeper realized that his hardship didn't prove anything about God. It just revealed who he was (and how we all are) without God. Because of his relationship with Christ, Jedidiah learned that he could always have peace and hope regardless of his circumstances. See page 58.

Journal

The following pages are provided for you to create your own journal. Each time you read *The Innkeeper's Journal* simply jot down some notes that will help you remember the setting, who was present, and what the story made you think about.

Acknowledgments

Without my wife, Michelle, this book would not exist. I wrote this story in 2017 for the culmination of a sermon series called, *The Innkeeper's Journal.* Christmas Eve was on Sunday that year, and we always have a very special candlelight service. I needed something a bit different so that the morning and evening services wouldn't feel similar. I decided to do a monologue and deliver it in full costume, something I'd only done twice before in three decades of pastoring. My aspirations were to memorize the script, but I just couldn't get it down. At the last minute, I opted to take my notes with me and prayed it wouldn't be a total disaster. There were no plans for a book, I just hoped to get through it without doing too much damage to Christmas Eve. Immediately after the service, Michelle enthusiastically said, "I want you to do that for our kids while they're home for Christmas." I had just dodged a bullet and couldn't imagine having to go through it again. But sure enough, she made me reapply the brown mascara all over my face to resemble a beard, stand by the firepit on our patio at night, and try to communicate this story to our adult children who thought it was as weird as I did. I survived and her encouragement somehow instilled a desire within me to create a book that might reframe some of our thinking about Christmas. Michelle, you are truly my soulmate, and this book would have never happened without you. Thank you for making this ride through life so enjoyable. I love you!

On December 24, 2017, Westgate Memorial Baptist Church became the first people to hear *The Innkeeper's Journal.* They were enthusiastic and encouraging about the presentation, but they're always that way so it wasn't a good barometer to gauge its merit. Dr. A.T. Robertson once said, "One of the best proofs of the inspiration of the Bible is that it has withstood so much preaching." Westgate has "withstood" two decades of my preaching and they still love me, so I call myself a very blessed man. It is an incredible church with an amazing staff. Thank you for letting me be your friend and pastor all these years! Love y'all and thanks for listening!

Michelle and I both have parents who taught us *shalom* long before we knew what it meant. Her parents, Loyd and Shirley Fannin, and my parents, Al and Martha McHenry, raised us in Christian homes where we grew to love God from an early age. These two couples helped shape who we are and what we've been able to do. They welcomed us into this life and periodically thought about taking us out of this life! They gave us what we believe is *life as God intended.* Thank you for giving us life, leading us into new life through Jesus Christ, and loving us as you have throughout this life. We love you!

A number of years ago I remember hearing, "Oh, you're Meagan and Myles' dad." When my children were much younger, they were "Raymond and Michelle's kids," but somewhere along the way their identity eclipsed ours. We wouldn't want it any other way. From as early as they can remember, I've regularly told them, "I love you and I'm proud of you!" That's never changed and never will. Meagan helped edit this book while working on her doctorate and offered some great insights that improved the final outcome. Myles is a successful businessman and entrepreneur, but he still thinks his dad has a little wisdom to offer, so his confidence in this book is deeply appreciated. Our son-in-law, Ben, is a wealth of information and could easily work the Genius Bar if he wasn't a minister. His help with technology was invaluable. Thanks for marrying our daughter and giving us grandkids. I do indeed love each of you, and I'm very proud of y'all!

After Hurricane Harvey devastated our area in 2017, Dr. David O. Dykes invited Michelle and me to spend a few days in Whistler with a group from his church. It was a wonderful gift of refreshment and reprieve from the day-to-day challenges that resulted from that catastrophic storm. While we were in Canada, I talked to him about a book I've labored with for years, *Relentless Pain: When the Hurt Won't Go Away.* He suggested I contact his editor because he thought she might be able to help me as well. That was a bonus gift because Mary Ann has walked with me through the whole process and took care of details I didn't even know existed. Somewhere in January of 2018 we decided *The Innkeeper's Journal* needed to be published first so I'll be thanking her again when we finish *Relentless Pain.* Everybody has a book idea, but unless you have someone like Mary Ann, it'll never end up in the library. It was her idea to make this book full color. I thought it'd be too expensive so I was thinking black and white. As the old adage goes, *thinking a bad idea is a good idea is still a bad idea.* David, thanks for introducing me to Mary Ann. Thank you, Mary Ann, for embracing my limited ideas and shaping them into something far more useful.

Each Sunday I look much better than I am because of the visual slides Matthew and Brittney Chandler create for my different sermon series. One day, Brittney pulled up a picture of me on her phone. It was a caricature drawing Matt made and it actually looks like me, at least in the face. It amazed me and introduced me to a whole other side of Matt Chandler. I asked him to join this experimental adventure and he willingly jumped on the train. He originally drew everything in black and white, because I unwisely asked him to do it that way. But then he came back and redrew all of the pictures in color (note Mary Ann's wise counsel above). His pictures make this book come alive. He had never done a project like this, and this was his first turn at doing color. Besides that, he drew it all on his iPad. I think Apple should send him a new iPad just for the free publicity he's giving them. Matt, you did a great job and I really appreciate your willingness to put that millennial spin on this old dinosaur's book. Matt and Brittney are church planters who supplement their ministry through their graphic design company *MC Designs* (matthewbchandler@icloud.com) and they'd be glad to make you look better too.

About 20 years ago, my father-in-law drew the cover of this book. He's a retired chemist with a great flair for art. He's drawn pictures of everyone in our family, including two family dogs. When he first drew the picture of Christ's birth in Bethlehem, he posted it online. It quickly rose to the top of Google's search results for such images! "Papa" has always supported and encouraged us in every new endeavor, and he's seen some pretty dumb ideas floated by his son-in-law. It's a great honor to have his artwork serve as the cover for this book. Thank you for agreeing to let me marry your daughter. It's made all the difference in my life.

Writing something that merges biblical truth with fiction is somewhat unsettling and can chip away at your confidence. I found affirmation for what I was attempting by reading John Piper's *The Innkeeper*, and Jim Denison's *The Myth and the Manger*. I am indebted to these great thinkers who are highly esteemed Christian leaders. Thank you for unknowingly giving me the confidence to continue on my odyssey of creating *The Innkeeper's Journal*.

This list of acknowledgments would not be complete without referencing the One for whom this book is written. Without Jesus Christ we are all helpless and hopeless, but with him we can be safe and secure. He really did come to give us life as God intended, and I will be eternally grateful that he did so. My life's goal is to *love God completely and encourage others to do the same* (see Matthew 22:37-40). To that end, please read *How To Experience Life As God Intended* on page 58. May you do as I have done and receive him as Lord and Savior.

P.S. If you would like to hear *The Innkeeper's Journal* monologue as it was originally delivered to the Westgate Memorial Baptist Church on December 24, 2017, visit **WestgateChurch.com.**

About the Author

Illustrated by Matthew Chandler

Raymond McHenry is a native Texan who grew up in Arizona. He's a graduate of Buena High School in Sierra Vista, Arizona and Grand Canyon College in Phoenix. Raymond also earned two degrees from Southwestern Baptist Theological Seminary, a Master of Divinity and a Doctor of Ministry. He's been a pastor for over thirty years: Gulf Meadows Baptist Church in Houston, Texas, (1987-1998) and Westgate Memorial Baptist Church in Beaumont, Texas, (1998-present). In 1991, he founded *In Other Words*, a research service that provides Christian leaders with humor, facts, quotes, and interesting true stories from current events and headline news. Visit **iows.net**.

Raymond met Michelle Fannin while they were both students at seminary and they married in 1986. They enjoy walking together, daily exercise, hiking, reading, skiing, golf, beaches and mountains, eating at Chick-fil-A, Carmela's, Pappadeaux and Carrabba's, and pursuing *shalom*. They have two grown children, a son-in-law, two beautiful granddaughters, and one goofy granddog.